LAUGH-LOVING FANS
DEMANDED MORE, SO SIGNET
PROUDLY PRESENTS
the sixth book collection of
cartoons starring the most popular
battling twosome in comics today—

THE LOCKHORNS
in

"Of Course I Love You—What Do I Know?"

By
BILL HOEST

More Big Laughs from SIGNET

- [ ] IT'S A ZIGGY WORLD by Tom Wilson. (#Y9504—$1.25)
- [ ] LIFE IS JUST A BUNCH OF ZIGGYS by Tom Wilson. (#Y8450—$1.25)
- [ ] ZIGGYS OF THE WORLD UNITE! by Tom Wilson. (#Y7800—$1.25)
- [ ] PLANTS ARE SOME OF MY FAVORITE PEOPLE by Tom Wilson. (#Y8055—$1.25)
- [ ] PETS ARE FRIENDS YOU LIKE WHO LIKE YOU RIGHT BACK by Tom Wilson. (#Y8264—$1.25)
- [ ] NEVER GET TOO PERSONALLY INVOLVED IN YOUR OWN LIFE by Tom Wilson. (#Y8986—$1.25)
- [ ] AL JAFFEE BLOWS A FUSE by Al Jaffee. (#E9549—$1.75)*
- [ ] AL JAFFEE MEETS HIS END by Al Jaffee. (#W8858—$1.50)*
- [ ] AL JAFFEE DRAWS A CROWD by Al Jaffee. (#W9275—$1.50)*
- [ ] AL JAFFEE SINKS TO A NEW LOW by Al Jaffee. (#E9757—$1.75)*
- [ ] AL JAFFEE GETS HIS JUST DESSERTS by Al Jaffee. (#E9838—$1.95)
- [ ] HIP KIDS' LETTERS FROM CAMP by Bill Adler. (#Q7107—95¢)
- [ ] MORE LETTERS FROM CAMP by Bill Adler. (#Y8580—$1.25)
- [ ] STILL MORE LETTERS FROM CAMP by Bill Adler. (#Y8946—$1.25)

* Price slightly higher in Canada

Buy them at your local bookstore or use this convenient coupon for ordering.

THE NEW AMERICAN LIBRARY, INC.,
P.O. Box 999, Bergenfield, New Jersey 07621

Please send me the SIGNET BOOKS I have checked above. I am enclosing
$_____ (please add 50¢ to this order to cover postage and handling).
Send check or money order—no cash or C.O.D.'s. Prices and numbers are
subject to change without notice.

Name _____

Address _____

City_____ State_____ Zip Code_____

Allow 4-6 weeks for delivery.
This offer is subject to withdrawal without notice.

"Of Course I Love You—What Do I Know?"

THE LOCKHORNS
By
BILL HOEST

A SIGNET BOOK
NEW AMERICAN LIBRARY
TIMES MIRROR

PUBLISHED BY
THE NEW AMERICAN LIBRARY
OF CANADA LIMITED

NAL BOOKS ARE AVAILABLE AT QUANTITY DISCOUNTS
WHEN USED TO PROMOTE PRODUCTS OR SERVICES. FOR
INFORMATION PLEASE WRITE TO PREMIUM MARKETING DIVISION,
THE NEW AMERICAN LIBRARY, INC., 1633 BROADWAY,
NEW YORK, NEW YORK 10019.

© 1978, 1979, 1980, 1981 King Features Syndicate, Inc.

All rights reserved

First Printing, August, 1981

2 3 4 5 6 7 8 9

SIGNET TRADEMARK REG. U.S. PAT. OFF. AND FOREIGN COUNTRIES
REGISTERED TRADEMARK - MARCA REGISTRADA
HECHO EN WINNIPEG, CANADA

SIGNET, SIGNET CLASSICS, MENTOR, PLUME, MERIDIAN
and NAL BOOKS are published in Canada by The New American
Library of Canada, Limited, Scarborough, Ontario

PRINTED IN CANADA
COVER PRINTED IN U.S.A.

"Of Course I Love You—What Do I Know?"

THE LOCKHORNS

"IT'S AN OLD FAMILY RECIPE, HANDED DOWN BY THE SURVIVORS."

"HE SAYS HE'S SOLEMN. I SAY HE'S SURLY!"

"NO, I DON'T KNOW HOW LONG WE'VE BEEN MARRIED... I'M NOT ONE TO BROOD."

"HOW ABOUT SINGING THE 'STAR-SPANGLED BANNER' AND CALLING IT A NIGHT?"

"DO YOU WANT TO HARASS MOTHER FOR A MINUTE?"

"HE'S RIGHT. YOUR NAGGING LACKS IMAGINATION."

"I'VE SPENT THE WHOLE DAY WITHOUT FOOD OR WATER!"

"HIS HEART ATTACK PILLS ARE IN HIS RIGHT-HAND JACKET POCKET."

"HOW COME YOU DON'T DRESS LIKE THAT?"

"WHAT TIME IS ZERO HOUR?"

"YOU'LL STOP YOUR LAUGHING WHEN YOU HEAR HOW MUCH I PAID FOR IT."

"WE HAD A HAPPY HOUR AFTER OUR WOMEN'S LIB MEETING."

"WELL, THANKS FOR HAVING US. IT WAS A WONDERFUL FOUR HOURS, TWELVE MINUTES AND TWENTY-ONE SECONDS."

"NO MORE FOR ME, THANKS, I'VE GOT TO BE GETTING HOME."

"WHAT DO YOU MEAN I NEVER TALK TO YOU AT THE BREAKFAST TABLE? DIDN'T I JUST SAY 'SHUT UP'?"

"LORETTA HAS A QUIET KIND OF BEAUTY ... IT HASN'T BEEN HEARD FROM IN YEARS!"

"AT THE STORE THEY SAID IT'S A GREAT COOKBOOK... HAS FIRE-FIGHTING HINTS IN THE BACK."

"CELEBRATE OUR ANNIVERSARY? DO THEY CELEBRATE PEARL HARBOR?"

"YOU HAD WORDS WITH YOUR WIFE AND SHE LEFT YOU? DO YOU REMEMBER WHAT THE WORDS WERE?"

"WHY DON'T WE LIGHT YOUR MEAT LOAF AND EAT THE CANDLES?"

"IT WILL BE HIGHER NEXT YEAR? I'M NOT GOING TO BUY IT NEXT YEAR, EITHER!"

"I'M NOT REALLY UNDECIDED. I'M JUST NOT SURE I WON'T CHANGE MY MIND."

"I HONESTLY CAN'T TELL THIS FROM REAL GROUND ROAST COFFEE. ARE YOU SURE IT'S CHICKEN BROTH?"

"SHE'S GOT MORE TALENT IN HER LITTLE FINGER THAN I HAVE IN MY BIG TOE."

"WALTZ A LITTLE FASTER, LEROY, THIS IS A FOX TROT!"

"IT ISN'T YOUR LACK OF THOUGHT FOR OUR ANNIVERSARY THAT BOTHERS ME ... IT'S THE LACK OF A GIFT!"

"OF COURSE I HAVE A HAPPY MARRIAGE. THE LOAN COMPANY IS HAPPY, THE CREDIT CARD COMPANY IS HAPPY, THE AUTO BODY SHOP IS HAPPY, ALL THE DEPARTMENT STORES..."

"IT *IS* RARE. YOU'RE LOOKING AT THE WRONG SIDE."

"WHEN DID YOU GIVE ME THE BEST YEARS OF YOUR LIFE?"

"THE ADVANTAGE OF HAVING A BUDGET IS THAT NOW WE *KNOW* WHY WE RUN OUT OF MONEY."

"GET THE BICARB. I NEED SOMETHING TO SETTLE YOUR HASH."

"HE CAN'T SLEEP WHEN HE GOES TO BED UNLESS HE HAS A NAP FIRST."

"IT'S FRIGHTENING TO REALIZE THAT WE MAY BE BETTER OFF NOW THAN WE'LL EVER BE!"

"TELL ME MORE ABOUT YOUR LATE-RUNNING BOARD MEETING!"

"THE STEAK MAY TASTE FUNNY. I DON'T THINK I GOT ALL THE FIRE EXTINGUISHER FLUID OFF IT."

"SO MUCH FOR PRO... HERE COMES CON."

"THERE ARE SO MANY DISHES TO WASH. WHY DON'T YOU DO HALF TONIGHT AND HALF TOMORROW?"

"IF THIS COFFEE WERE ANY STRONGER, YOU'D NEED A PRESCRIPTION."

"OUR BUDGET WILL WORK OUT FINE THIS MONTH. ALL I HAVE TO DO IS FIND SOME WAY TO SPEND $84.61."

"A MAN CHASED YOU? ... WHAT FOR?"

"... FOR WHAT WE ARE ABOUT TO RECEIVE ... LET THE SURVIVORS BE TRULY GRATEFUL."

"I REMEMBER GOING INTO THE BANK, MAKING A WITHDRAWAL ... THEN EVERYTHING WENT BLANK!"

"LEROY!"

"YOU'RE NOT REASONING WITH ME WHEN IT'S AT THE TOP OF YOUR VOICE!"

"... AND BLESS THIS FOOD WE ARE ABOUT TO RISK. AMEN."

"YOU'RE UP TO YOUR OLD TRICK OF PAYING ATTENTION WITHOUT LISTENING."

"AFTER ALL, LEROY, IT ISN'T AS IF I GAVE YOU BOTULISM ON PURPOSE!"

"THE FACIAL IS GUARANTEED FOR A WEEK OR UNTIL I WASH MY FACE, WHICHEVER COMES FIRST."

"WELL, OF COURSE I HAD TO TAKE A TAXI. THE CAR IS IN THE RIVER."

"WELL, THIS MEAT LOAF COULD BE WORSE... BUT I DON'T SEE HOW."

"CAN YOU THINK OF A BETTER WAY TO SPEND OUR ANNIVERSARY?"

"I'VE WORKED OUT A BUDGET WHERE WE CAN PAY AS WE GO, BUT WE WON'T HAVE ENOUGH TO GET BACK."

"HOW WAS I TO KNOW THE OATMEAL WOULD BE HOT? YOU USUALLY SERVE IT CHILLED!"

"THIS IS LEROY, MY ALLEGED BREADWINNER."

"NO, I WOULD NOT LIKE TO KNOW WHAT YOUR FRIEND, HELEN LENHART, MADE OF OUR LITTLE TIFF LAST NIGHT."

"AT ARTHUR'S BAR YOU MAY BE 'FEISTY,' BUT AROUND HERE YOU'RE JUST PLAIN QUARRELSOME."

"GOT SOMETHING TO WASH DOWN THIS SOUP?"

"YOU DON'T SEE ANYTHING OUTSTANDING ABOUT HER? WHERE ARE YOU LOOKING?"

"IF WE WERE TO REALLY COMMUNICATE, IT WOULD PROBABLY DRIVE US FARTHER APART."

"NO, LORETTA'S PARROT NEVER LEARNED TO TALK... IT NEVER GOT THE CHANCE."

"WHICH ARE THE ODDS AND WHICH ARE THE ENDS?"

"NEED ANY HELP?"

"DIAGNOSIS: TYPOGRAPHICAL ERROR IN MRS. LOCKHORN'S RECIPE BOOK."

"SHE'S NOT IN, AND IF MY LUCK HOLDS OUT, SHE WON'T BE FOR THE REST OF THE WEEK."

"WHY DON'T YOU INVITE MISS VON FLAME TO YOUR BIRTHDAY PARTY TO HELP YOU BLOW OUT ALL THOSE CANDLES?"

"I WAS LIVING LIFE TO THE FULLEST... AND IT OVERFLOWED!"

"CALL MY FATHER AND ASK HIM IF I CAN STILL GO INTO THE DRY GOODS BUSINESS."

"OH, COME NOW! WHAT HAS OUR BUDGET *EVER* HAD TO DO WITH THE MONEY WE SPEND?"

"LET'S GO TO THE EARLY MOVIE. I'LL HELP YOU PURGE THE DISHES."

"WANNA LAUGH? I BACKED OUT OF THE GARAGE AND FORGOT TO OPEN THE GARAGE DOOR."

"IT'S BEEN THREE DAYS AND HE SAYS MY BEEF STEW IS STILL STICKING TO HIS RIBS."

"I'D LIKE TO GO DOWNTOWN AND BUY A FEW THINGS. CAN I HAVE SEVEN HUNDRED DOLLARS?"

"IT'S AN EXPERIMENT. I MADE CHICKEN SOUP WITHOUT CHICKEN!"

"YOUR MOTHER JUST CALLED AND LEFT A MESSAGE."

"CANCEL ALL APPOINTMENTS, MISS MARGLIN, AND BREAK OUT MY BOTTLE OF LAFITTE ROTHSCHILD!"

"THE LAST THING YOU TOLD ME THIS MORNING WAS, 'HAVE A GOOD DAY'... AND, BY GEORGE, I SURE DID!"

"THIS IS MY FAVORITE DISH... VERY FAST RECOVERY TIME."

"KEEP UP THE GOOD WORK AND I'LL GIVE YOU A LETTER OF RECOMMENDATION IF WE EVER SPLIT."

"ACCORDING TO DOCTOR BLOG, I'M TO STAY OFF MY FEET, AND *YOU'RE* TO STAY OFF MY BACK!"

"LORETTA, BE REASONABLE! TAKE THE OLD SUITCASES!"

"DON'T EXPECT ANY SYMPATHY... I HAD AS BAD A TIME WITH YOU LAST NIGHT AS YOU'RE HAVING WITH YOU THIS MORNING."

"SO MUCH FOR YOUR CELEBRATED ABILITY TO POUR OIL ON TROUBLED WATERS."

"I RAN INTO AN OLD FRIEND WHO THOUGHT SHE COULD OUTSPEND ME!"

"I DON'T KNOW WHAT SHE'S RUNNING FOR... BUT SHE HAS MY VOTE!"

"YOU STAY HERE. I'LL GET HER NAME AND ADDRESS."

"A THOUSAND DOLLARS DOESN'T GO AS FAR AS IT USED TO."

"I WAS AWAKE HALF THE NIGHT, AND WHEN I FINALLY FELL ASLEEP I DREAMED I WAS AWAKE!"

"SURE THE COAT IS BECOMING TO YOU. BUT THE BILL WILL BE COMING TO ME!"

"HIDE THIS, LEROY ... IT'S MY CHRISTMAS PRESENT."

"I'M OF ENGLISH DESCENT. HE'S HALF SCOTCH AND HALF SODA."

"I GUESS YOU'LL BE NEEDING A PLACE TO STAY."

"OH, YEAH! WELL, WHEN IT COMES TO THAT, YOU'RE A POOR EXCUSE FOR COOKING!"

"HI, ARTHUR! ... JUST DROPPED IN FOR A MARRIAGE BREAK."

"YES, I THINK A NIGHT ON THE TOWN WOULD BE WONDERFUL, AND THERE'S NO REASON FOR YOU TO HURRY HOME."

"WELL, THIS CAKE CERTAINLY LOOKS... DURABLE!"

"NOT ONLY DOES SHE NAG, BUT ANYTHING I ACCOMPLISH SHE CREDITS TO HER NAGGING."

"YES, IT'S 'YOU' ALL RIGHT... AND THAT'S WHAT I DON'T LIKE ABOUT IT."

"I'M GOING TO LET YOU HAVE THE LAST WORD THIS TIME AND IT HAD BETTER BE SOMETHING NICE!"

"I SIMPLY SAID IT WAS THE BEST MEAL YOU EVER COOKED. I DIDN'T SAY ANYTHING ABOUT LIKING IT!"

"THIS WEEK LEROY CHANGED HIS GAME PLAN, FROM BEER TO BOURBON."

"HOW WOULD YOU LIKE YOUR ASPIRIN THIS MORNING... IN YOUR ORANGE JUICE OR IN YOUR SCRAMBLED EGGS?"

"HOW DO YOU KNOW WHEN YOU'RE DONE?"

"THIS IS AN OLD FAMILY RECIPE. IT'S BEEN POURED FROM SOME OF THE FINEST CASTLE TURRETS IN EUROPE."

"HOW COME YOU'RE ALWAYS 'FIRM' AND I'M ALWAYS 'PIGHEADED'?"

"I SEE YOU FIXED YOURSELF A BITE TO EAT!"

"INSTEAD OF SEPARATE VACATIONS, WHY DON'T WE VACATION TOGETHER AND LIVE SEPARATELY THE REST OF THE TIME?"

"BUT IF I OWN THE BOARDWALK, AND SHE'S IN JAIL, HOW CAN SHE TAKE ALL MY HOTELS ON ATLANTIC AVENUE AWAY FROM ME?"

"ONE GOOD THING ABOUT LORETTA'S PICNIC SPREAD... NO ANTS WILL BOTHER US."

"THEIR FOOD WAS TERRIBLE! I MIGHT AS WELL HAVE STAYED AT HOME!"

"IT WAS NOTHING. A MAN ASKED IF YOU COULD PLAY GOLF, AND I SAID NOT VERY WELL."

"AND WHEN I SNAP MY FINGERS, YOU WILL HAVE AN UNCONTROLLABLE URGE TO TAKE OUT THE GARBAGE!"

"WHAT MAKES YOU THINK SHE'LL DROWN IF YOU DON'T WATCH HER?"

"LOOK... I'LL LET YOU HAVE THE LAST WORD IF YOU'LL STOP RIGHT THERE!"

"MIND IF I PLAY THROUGH?"

"SO MUCH FOR YOUR BROTHER IN THE WHOLESALE BOAT BUSINESS."

"THE MOST MEMORABLE SIGHT ON OUR VACATION? I SUPPOSE IT WAS LEROY IN HIS BERMUDA SHORTS!"

"JUST A WORD OF WARNING, LORETTA! YOU'RE SPENDING MORE NOW THAN ALIMONY WOULD COST ME!"

"I WORKED OUT OUR BUDGET. WE CAN'T AFFORD FOOD *AND* SHELTER."

"LEROY DIDN'T ENJOY THE GRAND CANYON. IT DIDN'T HAVE A BAR."

"LEROY, I THINK I'M MISSING A BRIQUETTE!"

**"AVOID ALL FORMS OF EXCITEMENT?
YOU MEAN, NO NAPS?"**

"OF COURSE IT'S YOUR FAULT. THE ONLY REASON I'M LATE IS THAT YOU GOT HERE BEFORE ME!"

"DIDN'T I SEE THIS RECIPE IN SOME FAMOUS BOOK? AGATHA CHRISTIE OR SHERLOCK HOLMES?"

"YOU SHOULDN'T MONOPOLIZE MISS VON FLAME LIKE THAT. GIVE SOME OTHER HUSBAND A CHANCE TO MAKE A FOOL OF HIMSELF."

"DON'T TELL ME THE MYSTERIOUS PHANTOM FENDER-SMASHER HAS STRUCK AGAIN!"

"HER LUGGAGE GOT HERE OKAY, BUT SOMEHOW YOUR MOTHER WAS FLOWN TO PEORIA."

"IF THE ROACH POISON DOESN'T WORK, TRY SOME OF THIS COFFEE ON THEM!"

"LORETTA HAS HER FILE OF RECIPES AND I HAVE MY FILE OF ANTIDOTES."

"WELCOME HOME, LEROY! YOU ALMOST MISSED YOUR BIRTHDAY CELEBRATION!"

"BEING CONSIDERATE IS LEROY'S SECOND NATURE. UNFORTUNATELY, BEING *IN*CONSIDERATE IS HIS FIRST."

"YOU KNOW HOW THEY MADE CARVER A ONE-WAY STREET? I JUST FOUND OUT WHICH WAY."

"DON'T GET YOUR HOPES UP. I'M CLEARING MY THROAT, NOT CHOKING."

"IT'S ALL RIGHT, MISS. AT HIS AGE IT'S NICE TO SEE HIM TAKE AN INTEREST IN *SOMETHING!*"

"IF IT WERE UP TO YOU, OUR CREDIT WOULD JUST LAY THERE AND RUST."

"AND JUST LAST NIGHT YOU WERE SINGING, 'HAPPY DAYS ARE HERE AGAIN'!"

"LEROY HAS THE RUSSIAN FLU. HE SAYS THE ONLY THING THAT CURES IT IS VODKA."

"WE WERE ABOUT TO MAKE BOTH ENDS MEET WHEN SOMETHING SNAPPED IN THE MIDDLE."

"SURE I KNOW MONEY DOESN'T GROW ON TREES! DID YOU KNOW *DRESSES* DON'T GROW ON TREES?"

"I THINK THERE'S LESS TO HER THAN MEETS THE EYE!"

"I WISH YOU WOULDN'T DIGRESS WHEN YOU'RE BEATING AROUND THE BUSH!"

"JUST GOT THROUGH CUTTING THE GRASS... NOW, IN A MINUTE, I'LL DO OURS."

"YOU SAID HELEN LENHART NEVER RETURNED YOUR COOKBOOK. I'M CALLING TO THANK HER."

"IF TODAY IS FRIDAY, THEN THIS MUST BE FISH."

"BOY, I KNEW THERE WERE SOME BIG ONES IN HERE! DID YOU HEAR THAT SPLASH?"

"I GOT YOUR MOTHER SOME FLIGHT INSURANCE. I HOPE IT WAS MONEY WELL SPENT."

"THE AVERAGE WOMAN WOULD RATHER HAVE BEAUTY THAN BRAINS BECAUSE THE AVERAGE MAN CAN *SEE* BETTER THAN HE CAN *THINK!*"

"EXCUSE ME, MISS HOTCHKISS, WOULD YOU MIND SUNNING YOURSELF IN THE WILSONS' YARD FOR A WHILE? THE *OTHER* SIDE OF OUR LAWN NEEDS WEEDING, TOO!"

"OH, STOP SCREAMING! WHEN YOU'VE SEEN ONE TRIPLE PLAY YOU'VE SEEN THEM ALL!"

"MOST OF OUR GROUP ARE REAL TOURISTS, BUT YOU... YOU JUST CAME TO HAVE A GOOD TIME!"

"DON'T WORRY, HERB. LORETTA KNOWS YOU'RE COMING FOR DINNER. WE HAD IT OUT LAST NIGHT."

"OH, BOY! OUR MEMBERSHIP CARDS TO THE GRASSY MEADOW NUDIST CAMP FINALLY CAME!"

"AND NOW, LORETTA'S REBUTTAL TO GRACIOUS LIVING!"

"I APPRECIATE YOUR TRYING TO SOBER ME UP, LORETTA, BUT PUTTING AN OLIVE IN BLACK COFFEE DOESN'T FOOL *ME*!"

"I DON'T KNOW WHERE SHE WENT. SHE JUST SCREAMED THAT HER CREDIT CARD EXPIRES TODAY, AND DASHED OUT THE DOOR."

"YOU'RE EATING THE CENTERPIECE."

"OH, LEROY'S A GOOD PROVIDER... IF YOU LIKE BOOZE."

"WHEN WE MOVED, THE TELEPHONE COMPANY RETIRED OUR OLD NUMBER."

"ASIDE FROM YOUR BROKEN TOOTH, HOW WAS DINNER?"

"LEFTOVER FROM WHAT... DINNER AT THE BORGIAS'?"

"HE MET HER THE USUAL WAY... OPENED HIS WALLET AND THERE SHE WAS."

"I HAVE AMNESIA... I CAN'T REMEMBER WHY I GOT MARRIED!"

"I HOPE YOU DON'T HOLD A GRUDGE."

"OKAY, SO YOU'VE PROVED YOUR POINT! WHAT KIND OF LOGIC IS THAT?"